Y0-BPU-120

# Counting Your Blessings

# Counting Your Blessings

A Little Book
About the Joys of Life
By Edward Cunningham

Illustrated by Kathy Spahr

HALLMARK EDITIONS

# Counting Your Blessings

Life holds so many blessings,
both large and small,
we can't begin to count them all....

....and just thinking of blessings
that we possess
can fill our hearts with
thankfulness.

A memory that lingers forever after
is a wonderful blessing....

....and so is laughter!

Some blessings are surprises,
like a secret dream come true
that makes the world a happier place....

....and you a happier you!

And sometimes
when you're downhearted,
you'll find blessings in disguise....

....like times when showers
turn to flowers
right before your eyes!

There's the blessing
of learning something new
and growing a little each day....

and the blessing of a faith
that lights your path
and guides you on your way.

It's a blessing having a family
that understands and cares....

and home is a blessing
to cherish,
for happiness lives there.

A friend who is on your side
through happiness and tears....

is a very precious blessing
you can treasure
through the years.

But of all your blessings,
large and small,
there's one that stands apart....

it's the blessing of love.
Life takes on more meaning
when love comes
to your heart.

You'll find some of
your happiest times
have only begun....

when the blessing of love
is sent from above
and the two of you truly are one.

And the joys that you have had
are just a preview of....

a future filled with blessings
of happiness and love.

So whenever you
count your blessings,
chances are you'll be surprised
to find how many more you have
than you ever realized!